Activities and Projects, Chapters 1-9

Intro to Business

SIXTH EDITION

Les R. Dlabay

James L. Burrow

Steven A. Eggland

Australia · Brazil · Canada · Mexico · Singapore · Spain · United Kingdom · United States

Intro to Business, 6th edition
Activities and Projects, Chapters 1-9

Dlabay, Burrow, Eggland

VP/Editorial Director
Jack W. Calhoun

VP/Editor-in-Chief
Karen Schmohe

Executive Editor
Eve Lewis

Project Manager
Enid Nagel

Production Manager
Patricia Matthews Boies

Ancillary Coordinator
Kelly Resch

VP/Director of Marketing
Carol Volz

Senior Marketing Manager
Nancy Long

Marketing Coordinator
Angela A. Russo

Manufacturing Coordinator
Kevin Kluck

Art Director
Michelle Kunkler

Editorial Assistant
Linda Keith

Cover Designer
Liz Harasymczuk Design

Cover Photo Source
© Nikolai Punin/Stock Illustrati

Printer
Edwards Brothers
Ann Arbor, MI

Printed in the United States of America
1 2 3 4 5 08 07 06 05

0-538-44076-7

For more information about ou products, contact us at:

Thomson Higher Education
5191 Natorp Boulevard
Mason, OH 45040
USA

Activities and Projects, Chapters 1-9

CONTENTS

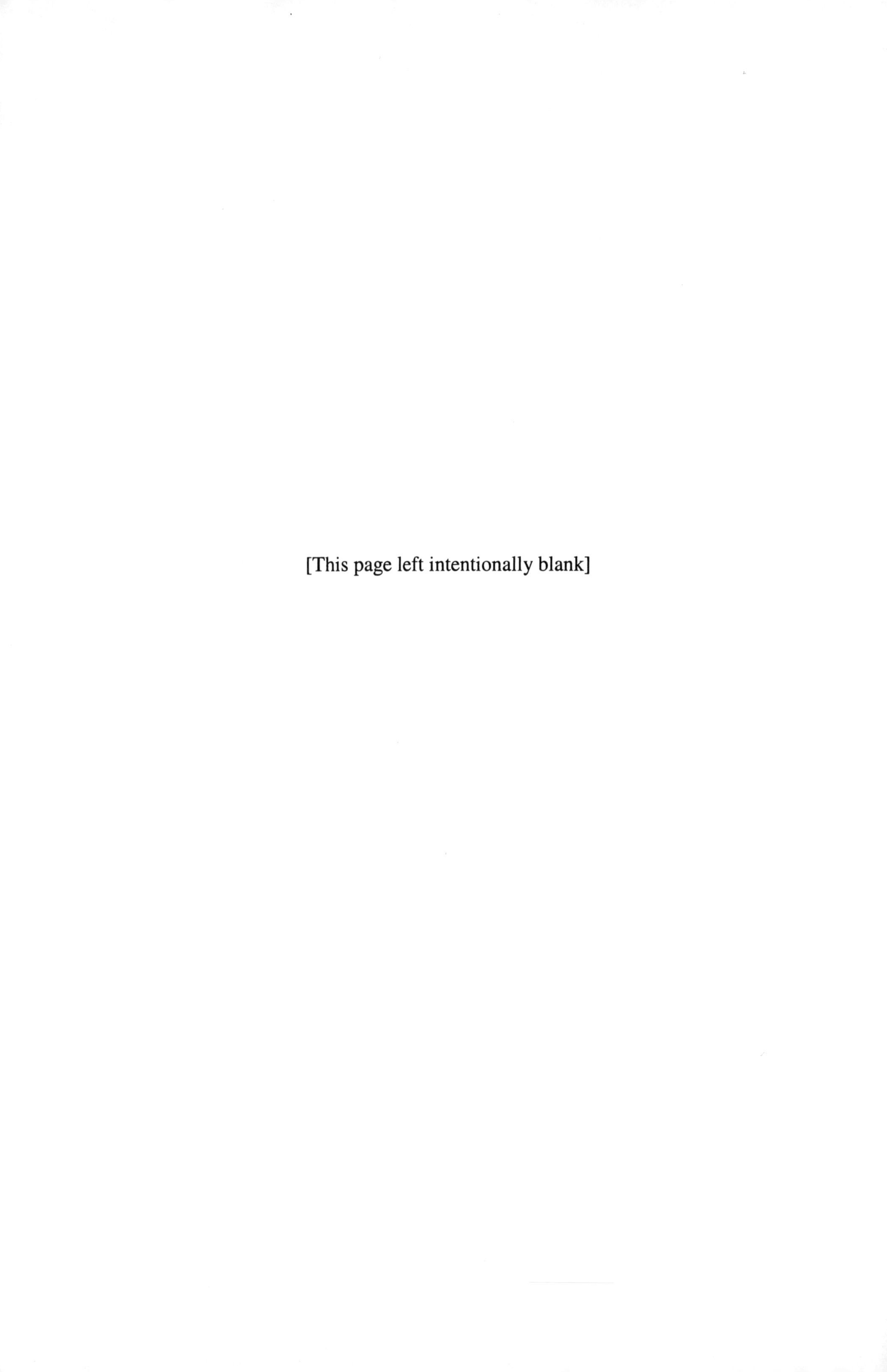

[This page left intentionally blank]

Name ______________________ Class ______________ Date ______________

Chapter 1 Study Guide Economic Decisions and Systems

Part 1 True or False

Directions Place a *T* for True or an *F* for False in the Answers column to show whether each of the following statements is true or false.

Answers

1. A compact disc player is an example of a need. 1.______
2. Tangible products you can purchase to meet your wants and needs are called goods. 2.______
3. When you decide to buy a jacket instead of a concert ticket, you are making a tradeoff. 3.______
4. Capitalism is another name for a traditional economic system. 4.______
5. Competition forces businesses to search for new ways to satisfy customers' wants and needs. 5.______
6. The market price for a product is the point where demand exceeds supply. 6.______
7. Economists predict future changes in the economy. 7.______
8. China is the largest producer of goods and services in the world. 8.______

Part 2 Multiple Choice

Directions In the Answers column, write the letter that represents the word, or group of words, that correctly completes the statement.

Answers

9. The basic economic problem is (a) having unlimited wants and needs but limited economic resources (b) deciding what goods and services to produce (c) identifying the goods and services available to you (d) determining how to satisfy needs and wants. 9.______
10. An important principle of the U.S. economic system is (a) the right to private property (b) the freedom of choice (c) competition (d) all of the above. 10.______
11. If freezing weather damages orange crops in Florida (a) the demand for oranges will decrease (b) the price of oranges will increase (c) the supply of oranges will remain unchanged (d) the price of orange juice will decrease. 11.______
12. Water, air, and minerals are examples of (a) consumer resources (b) natural resources (c) capital resources (d) human resources. 12.______
13. If you decide to purchase a DVD of your favorite movie instead of a pair of jeans, the value of the jeans is the (a) market price (b) profit (c) opportunity cost (d) tradeoff price 13.______

Part 3 Matching

Directions In the Answers column indicate which economic system is best described by each statement.

A. controlled economy C. traditional economy

B. market economy D. mixed economy

Answers

14. Resources are owned and controlled by the people of the country. 14.______
15. The government decides what and how goods are produced. 15.______
16. Workers often use hand tools and readily available natural resources. 16.______
17. As countries become more developed, they often adopt this economic system. 17.______
18. Consumers base their decisions on their own self-interest. 18.______

Part 4 Activities

19. Review your own recent purchases and observe newspaper ads or store signs that feature price changes. In the following table, list five examples of products or services for which you have noticed price changes. Identify the product or service; show whether the price change was an increase or decrease; and identify the reason for the price change.

Product or Service	Price Increase or Decrease?	Reason for Price Change

20. The graph below represents the supply and demand for music CDs. Using the data provided in this graph, write a paragraph discussing the relationship between supply and demand. Why is it important for businesses to have this type of information when producing or selling a product? Based on the information provided, what is the market price for music CDs?

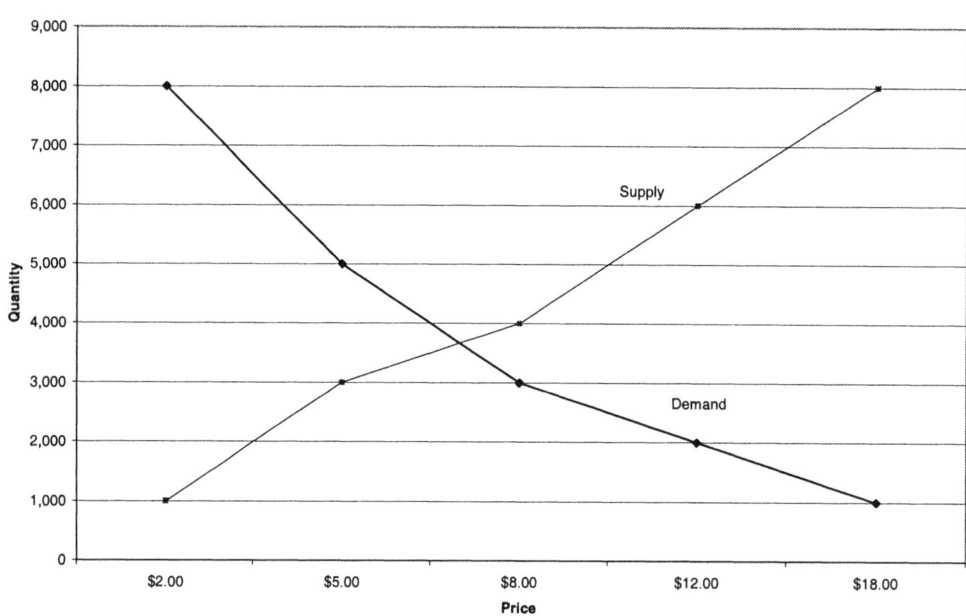

Name ______________________ Class ______________ Date ______________

21. For the past three years, Marci and Jeff have operated a small bake shop in their suburban neighborhood. Through their hard work and positive word-of-mouth advertising, the business has grown. Now Marci and Jeff are exploring ways to expand the business. They like their current location and have built a loyal customer base there, so they do not want to relocate. Since it is not possible to enlarge their current bake shop, they have considered opening a second location in another part of town. This would give their business exposure to new customers, but it would require them to lease space, purchase ovens and other equipment, and hire and train new employees. Also, one of them probably would have to move to the new location to oversee operations. Another option is for Marci and Jeff to sell their baked goods to other businesses in town, such as restaurants and small grocery stores, for resale to their customers. That option would allow both Marci and Jeff to remain in their current location, but it would require them to upgrade their current ovens and add additional employees to handle the increased production. They also would need to hire a salesman to contact local companies and purchase a delivery vehicle and hire a driver to deliver the baked goods to locations around town. Use the steps in the decision-making process to help Marci and Jeff decide which option to pursue.

What is the problem Marci and Jeff are facing?

What are the choices that Marci and Jeff must consider?

What are the advantages and disadvantages of each choice?

Which choice do you think is best for Marci and Jeff and why?

What should Marci and Jeff do once they have decided how they will expand their business?

[This page left intentionally blank]

Name ______________________ Class ______________ Date ______________

Chapter 2 Study Guide Economic Activity

Part 1 Unscramble

Directions Unscramble the following vocabulary words that were discussed in Chapter 2.

Answers

1. rutviiopdcyt — 1. ____________
2. ctsko — 2. ____________
3. yitqeu — 3. ____________
4. orseisnec — 4. ____________
5. ladfetnoi — 5. ____________
6. ertinsetetar (2 words) — 6. ____________
7. spytopirer — 7. ____________
8. prixcedine (2 words) — 8. ____________
9. lftiinano — 9. ____________
10. fdegtubitedci (2 words) — 10. ____________
11. vycrereo — 11. ____________
12. nycbeusciless (2 words) — 12. ____________

Part 2 Matching

Directions In the Answers column, write the word or phrase from Part 1 above that correctly matches each statement below.

Answers

13. A period in which most people who want to work have a job, wages are good, businesses are producing a record number of goods, and the rate of gross domestic product (GDP) growth is increasing — 13. ____________
14. Can be increased by an improvement in management techniques — 14. ____________
15. Although there is a decrease in prices, people have less money to buy products — 15. ____________
16. A situation where a government spends more money than it takes in over a period of time — 16. ____________
17. A period in which unemployment begins to rise, demand begins to decrease, and businesses lower production — 17. ____________
18. An increase in prices and a decrease in the buying power of the dollar — 18. ____________
19. Represents the cost of money — 19. ____________
20. A phase represented by an increase in employment, demand for goods, and the GDP — 20. ____________
21. Movement of the economy from one condition to another — 21. ____________
22. Represents ownership in a corporation — 22. ____________

Part 3 Name That Measure

Directions In the Answers column match the following economic measures with their descriptions.

A.	gross domestic product (GDP)	C.	Consumer Price Index (CPI)
B.	unemployment rate	D.	retail sales

Answers

23. Compares the prices of a group of selected items each year to some earlier year 23.____
24. The total dollar value of all final goods and services produced each year in a country 24.____
25. Monthly measure of the sales of durable and nondurable goods bought by consumers 25.____
26. The most widely used measure of national output 26.____
27. The percentage of people in the labor force who are willing to work, are looking for work but are unable to find work 27.____

Part 4 Activities

28. Business journals and newspapers regularly publish articles analyzing data that has been compiled by the government to examine the relative health of the economy. Conduct research to locate a current article dealing with one of the leading economic indicators, such as gross domestic product, consumer spending, interest rates, common stock prices, or unemployment rates. Read the article and write a report that addresses the issues listed below. Attach a copy of the article to your report.

    The cover sheet should include:

    Title of the article

    Source

    Date

    Your name

    Class

    The body of the report should present:

    A summary of the article.

    Discussion of how this information will affect you, your family, and your community.

    Discussion of how this information will affect local businesses, their employees, and the economy in general.

    The conclusion of the report should present:

    Your opinion of the impact this information will have on the economy in the future.

    Your thoughts on the value of the information in the article.

Name ______________________ Class ______________ Date ______________

29. Employment statistics can relate valuable information about the economy. In times of prosperity, employment usually increases. However, in some industries, jobs may decrease even in times of prosperity if the production of goods to satisfy needs and wants is changing. The 2004 Statistical Abstract of the United States contains the following employment data for sectors of the U.S. economy from 2000 through 2003.

	EMPLOYMENT (in millions)		PERCENTAGE OF CHANGE	RANK IN NO. OF JOBS
INDUSTRY	2000	2003		
Wholesale/Retail	20.0	20.7	______	______
Finance/Real Estate	9.4	9.7	______	______
Transportation and Utilities	7.4	7.0	______	______
Construction	9.9	10.1	______	______
Manufacturing	19.6	16.9	______	______
Education and Health Services	26.2	28.3	______	______
Professional, Business and other Services	20.1	20.7	______	______

1. Calculate the percentage of change in each of the categories and record it in the table. Round off your answers to the nearest percent.

2. Was there a decrease in employment in any category? If so, which one(s)?

____

3. Rank the categories based on the total number of people employed in each industry in 2003. Most people were employed in which category?

____

4. Which category experienced the greatest percentage of increase? How many people does that percentage of increase represent?

____

5. What conclusions about the U.S. economy can you draw from this table?

____

[This page left intentionally blank]

Name ______________________ Class ______________ Date ______________

Chapter 3 Study Guide Business in the Global Economy

Part 1 Yes or No

Directions Indicate your answer to each of the following questions by placing a check mark on the line under *yes* or *no* at the right.

	Yes	No
1. Is foreign debt the amount of money that other countries owe the United States?	____	____
2. If a country imports more than it exports, does it have a trade deficit?	____	____
3. Does supply and demand affect the exchange rate?	____	____
4. Does a country's infrastructure refer to its climate and natural resources?	____	____
5. Are tariffs on certain goods used to restrict free trade?	____	____
6. Is the North American Free Trade Agreement (NAFTA) an agreement created by the United States, Mexico, and Japan?	____	____
7. Does licensing have a low financial investment and a high potential financial return?	____	____
8. Are franchise agreements popular with fast-food companies such as McDonald's, Wendy's, and Burger King?	____	____

Part 2 Completion

Directions In the Answers column, write the word or words needed to complete each sentence.

	Answers
9. The primary effects on a country's level of economic development are its literacy level, agricultural dependency, and (?).	9. ______________
10. Making, buying, and selling goods and services within a country is referred to as (?).	10. ______________
11. When a country can produce a particular good or service at a lower cost than other countries, a(n) (?) exists.	11. ______________
12. The (?) is the value of currency in one country compared with the value of currency in another.	12. ______________
13. Trade barriers can include (?), tariffs, and embargoes.	13. ______________
14. An agreement between two or more companies to work together on a business project is called a(n) (?).	14. ______________
15. A(n) (?) is also known as an economic community.	15. ______________

Part 3 Matching

Directions In the Answers column indicate which international trade organization or agreement is best described by each statement.

A. World Trade Organization (WTO)
C. North American Free Trade Agreement (NAFTA)
B. The World Bank
D. The International Monetary Fund (IMF)

		Answers
16.	Maintains a system of world trade and exchange rates	16.____
17.	Created after World War II to provide loans for rebuilding	17.____
18.	Settles trade disputes and enforces free-trade agreements between member countries	18.____
19.	Key function is to provide economic aid to less developed countries	19.____
20.	Does away with taxes on goods traded among the member countries	20.____

Part 4 Activities

21. The currency exchange rate changes constantly based on factors such as a country's balance of payments, economic conditions, and political stability. Figure 3-4 shows the values of currencies in several countries in relation to the U.S. dollar (USD). Visit the web site for the Universal Currency Converter at http://www.xe.com/ucc/ and check the value of those currencies today. Fill in the blanks to indicate each currency's units per USD and value in USD. Compare your findings with the values provided in Figure 3-4, and place a check mark in the appropriate blank to indicate whether the value of the USD has increased or decreased in relation to each of the other currencies.

Country	Currency	Units per USD	Value in USD	Increase	Decrease
Britain	pound				
Brazil	real				
Canada	dollar				
European Union	euro				
Japan	yen				
Saudi Arabia	riyal				
South Africa	rand				
South Korea	won				
Venezuela	bolivar				

Name ______________________________ Class ____________________ Date ____________________

22. Numerous items that you buy and use every day are produced in other countries, primarily due to lower production and labor costs. Many American companies maintain manufacturing facilities outside of the United States in order to remain competitive in the marketplace by reducing their costs of production. As more companies move all or part of their business operations outside of the United States, it can have both positive and negative effects on the economies in the U.S. as well as in the host country. In the space below, list some of the positive and negative effects on both economies.

Positive Effects on the United States	**Negative Effects on the United States**

Positive Effects on the Host Country	**Negative Effects on the Host Country**

23. When it comes to world trade, most people have a strong opinion. Some people believe that too many American jobs are being lost to overseas labor markets. Others believe that international trade actually creates new jobs in the United States. Now that you have completed this chapter, you should better understand the value of international trading, but how do others feel about world trade? Talk to at least five (5) people you know and ask their opinions. Do not record their names, but bring the results of your survey to class to share. Here are some questions that you might ask.

1. Do you believe there are advantages for the United States in trading with other nations? Why or why not?
2. Do you think international trading increases an understanding of other cultures? If so, how?
3. Do you believe that American jobs are lost because of importing? Why or why not?
4. Do you believe that the North American Free Trade Agreement (NAFTA) and other free trade agreements are good for the U.S. economy? Why or why not?
5. Do you think the United States should place an embargo on certain goods or on goods from certain countries? If so, what goods, what countries, and for what reasons?
6. Do you buy goods made in other countries? If so, what do you buy and why?
7. Do you think it is possible in today's marketplace to only "Buy American"? Why or why not?
8. If you are employed, is your employer involved in international trade? If so, in what way?

[This page left intentionally blank]

Name ______________________________ Class ____________________ Date ____________________

Chapter 4 Study Guide Social Responsibility of Business and Government

Part 1 True or False

Directions Place a *T* for True or an *F* for False in the Answers column to show whether each of the following statements is true or false.

Answers

1. To be valid and enforceable, contracts must be in writing and signed by both parties. 1.______
2. A logo is a trademark linked with a specific company or product. 2.______
3. The Age Discrimination in Employment Act protects people once they reach age 65. 3.______
4. Intrastate commerce involves companies doing business in only one state. 4.______
5. When a business controls the market for a product or service, it has a monopoly. 5.______
6. Microsoft Corporation is the single largest employer in the United States. 6.______
7. The government's sole source of income is taxes, such as income, property, and sales taxes. 7.______
8. A business's duty to contribute to the well-being of the community is its social responsibility. 8.______

Part 2 Matching

Directions In the Answers column, write the letter that represents the word, or group of words, that correctly completes the statement.

			Answers
9.	Results in an unfair benefit	A. antitrust laws	9.______
10.	Cannot be replaced once it has been used up	B. code of ethics	10.______
11.	Protects the work of authors, composers, and artists	C. non-renewable resource	11.______
12.	Saves scarce natural resources	D. public utility	12.______
13.	Guides the actions of employees	E. copyright	13.______
14.	Prevent unfair business practices	F. conservation	14.______
15.	Supplies a product or service vital to all people	G. conflict of interest	15.______

Part 3 Multiple Choice

Directions In the Answers column indicate which government agency is best described by each statement.

A. Environmental Protection Agency (EPA)
B. Department of Commerce
C. Small Business Administration (SBA)
D. Occupational Safety and Health Administration (OSHA)

Answers

16. Regulates safety standards 16.______
17. Monitors and enforces standards for water and air quality 17.______
18. Provides information to help companies make good business decisions 18.______
19. Helps new businesses get started by offering business loans 19.______
20. Works closely with businesses to reduce pollution 20.______

Part 4 Activities

21. Government plays an important role in many areas of society. In Column 1 below are five roles in which government is involved. In Column 2 list several government activities for each role the government play in our economy. The first item is provided as an example. See if you can add to the list.

COLUMN 1	COLUMN 2
providing services for members of society	***Example: highways***
protecting citizens, consumers, businesses, and workers	
regulating utilities and promoting competition	
providing information and support	
buying goods and services	

22. Ian Broderick is the president and chief executive officer of a small printing company of about 400 employees. Although the business is small, it has grown steadily over the past few years, and Mr. Broderick and other company executives think it is time to formalize the company's commitment to ethical business practices. You have been asked to write a code of ethics for Broderick Printing Company that will address topics such as honesty, courtesy, and confidentiality as well as rules of conduct for dealing with customers and coworkers. You may want to review the American Express Blue Box Values in Figure 4-1 as a guide. Be sure to give your code of ethics an appropriate title.

23. Employee wellness programs benefit both employers and employees. Healthier workers are more productive and miss fewer days from work due to illness. Conduct a brief survey among people you know who work in various businesses and compile a list of the programs provided by their employers. You may also want to ask them what programs they would like to see offered in the future that currently are not available at their place of employment.

[This page left intentionally blank]

Name ______________________ Class ______________ Date ______________

Chapter 5 Study Guide Business Organization

Part 1 Agree or Disagree

Directions Indicate whether you agree or disagree with each of the following statements by placing a check mark in the column at the right.

	Agree	Disagree
1. The most important role of business is to provide employment for people.	______	______
2. Producers use resources to make things that are needed by others.	______	______
3. Service businesses represent the fastest growing segment of the economy.	______	______
4. Nonprofit corporations do not pay corporate income taxes.	______	______
5. An S-corporation is a corporation involved in the service industry.	______	______
6. A mission statement defines what the business wants to achieve.	______	______
7. In a matrix organization structure, work is arranged around business functions.	______	______
8. An organizational chart is a detailed list of job duties and responsibilities.	______	______

Part 2 Short Answer

Directions In the Answers column, write the word or words that best describes each statement below.

	Answers
9. The large number of people born between 1946 and 1964	9. ______________
10. A statement of results a businesses plans to achieve	10. ______________
11. Businesses involved in selling goods produced by others	11. ______________
12. The number of people assigned to a specific work task or manager	12. ______________
13. A business organized by two or more other businesses for a limited time	13. ______________
14. Someone who has no contract for long-term employment	14. ______________
15. A business owned by members and managed in their interest	15. ______________

Part 3 Organizational Structures

Directions In the Answers column, please a F for Functional and an M for Matrix to indicate which organizational structure is best described by each statement.

	Answers
16. All people with jobs related to a specific function work together.	16. ______
17. People work with others who have the same skills.	17. ______
18. Assignments may be temporary or long-term.	18. ______
19. People often have little interaction with people in other parts of the business.	19. ______
20. Work is structured around specific projects, products, or customer groups.	20. ______
21. People with varied backgrounds work together to serve the customer.	21. ______
22. Work is arranged within main business functions such as production and marketing.	22. ______

Part 4 Activities

23. Listed below are some statements about the three major forms of business ownership. Place a check mark in the column that identifies the form of business ownership described by each statement. Some statements may apply to more than one type of business ownership.

Characteristics	Sole Proprietorship	Partnership	Corporation
1. Owned and controlled by two or more people	______	______	______
2. A written agreement defines ownership.	______	______	______
3. Owned and run by one person	______	______	______
4. Shareholders have a voice in business decisions.	______	______	______
5. No protection for personal assets	______	______	______
6. Managed by a board of directors	______	______	______
7. Usually must be dissolved if an owner leaves	______	______	______
8. The easiest form of business to start and run	______	______	______
9. Protects the liability of owners	______	______	______
10. Business income is taxed as personal income	______	______	______
11. Two or more people can invest in the business	______	______	______
12. Must create bylaws or operating procedures	______	______	______
13. Does not even require a business name	______	______	______
14. The majority of U.S. businesses	______	______	______
15. Must register the business name and the names of all owners.	______	______	______

24. A franchise is a written contract that gives a business the right to sell products and services in a specific way within a given area. A wide variety of familiar businesses within your community operate as franchises, including fast-food restaurants, pizza shops, motels, commercial cleaning companies, and weight loss centers. Select a franchise business and conduct research to learn more about the franchise opportunities.

What start-up costs and franchise fees (percentage of profits) are franchisees required to pay?

____

What type of operating assistance does the franchiser provide?

____

What would be the benefits of investing in the franchise instead of starting a similar business on your own?

____

____

Name ____________________ Class ____________________ Date ____________________

25. Each day you deal with many different types of businesses, including producers that create the products and services used by others, intermediaries that sell those goods and services to consumers and businesses, and service businesses that offer intangible activities that are consumed by others. In each of the following scenarios, identify the types of businesses involved.

1. Rob Lopez wants to have three rooms in his home painted. He visits the local Home Depot store, selects the paint colors from samples available in the Paint Department and purchases six gallons of Glidden brand paint, which he estimates is sufficient to paint the rooms. After paying for the paint, Rob stops by the service counter and looks at a list of independent painting contractors. He decides to contact several of the contractors to request estimates on painting the rooms.

____

____

2. Molly Russell loves to cook and has finally turned her hobby into a business by opening Molly's Gourmet Meals, producing complete gourmet meals that are fully cooked and ready to heat and eat. Because she believes in using the finest and freshest ingredients, Molly purchases all of her produce from a small farm close to her home. Molly sells her gourmet meals through various outlets, including the deli departments at several local supermarkets. Because she needs to remain in the kitchen overseeing production, Molly has contracted with another small business person, Stephen Daily of Daily Deliveries, to deliver the meals to the supermarkets.

____

____

____

3. Jeff Martin owns a mobile dog grooming business, On the Go Grooming, which allows customers to conveniently have their pets groomed at home. Jeff purchased three vans from a local dealership and took them to Custom Car Creations to have sinks, drying stations, and grooming stations added to allow him and his staff to shampoo, dry, and clip dogs right in the customer's driveway. Each van also contains built-in cabinets, which are stocked with an assortment of animal care products, which Jeff orders in bulk from the manufacturer. Because many of his customers have begun asking if they can purchase some of the pet care products for use at home, Jeff recently began ordering some of the products in smaller packages to sell to customers.

____

____

____

____

[This page left intentionally blank]

Name ____________________ Class ____________ Date ____________

Chapter 6 Study Guide Entrepreneurship and Small Business Management

Part 1 True or False

Directions Place a *T* for True or an *F* for False in the Answers column to show whether each of the following statements is true or false.

		Answers
1.	An independent business with 200 employees is considered a small business.	1. ______
2.	Most new business owners obtain start-up money to finance their business from banks.	2. ______
3.	Small businesses employ only 10 percent of U.S. workers.	3. ______
4.	Successful entrepreneurs have many personal characteristics in common.	4. ______
5.	An entrepreneur is someone who takes a risk by starting his own business.	5. ______
6.	Start-up financing is money needed to pay current operating costs of the business.	6. ______
7.	One of the main reasons that businesses started by entrepreneurs fail is inadequate capital.	7. ______
8.	A business plan includes a description of the strengths and weakness of competitors.	8. ______

Part 2 Matching

Directions In the Answers column, write the letter that represents the word, or group of words, that correctly matches the statement.

			Answers
9.	The process of starting, organizing, and managing a business	A. improvement	9. ______
10.	A brand new invention	B. venture capital	10. ______
11.	A written description of the business idea	C. mission statement	11. ______
12.	Money provided by large investors to finance new businesses	D. entrepreneurship	12. ______
13.	A change that increases the usefulness of a product	E. innovation	13. ______
		F. business plan	

Part 3 Multiple Choice

Directions Identify the type of financing being described by each of the statements by placing a check mark in the correct column.

		Start-up	Short-Term	Long-Term
14.	Money to pay for current operating costs of the business	______	______	______
15.	Purchase of the equipment to open a business	______	______	______
16.	Money used to open the business	______	______	______
17.	Financing that is obtained for less than a year	______	______	______
18.	The license to operate a business	______	______	______
19.	Large amounts of money paid over many years	______	______	______
20.	The land that the business is built on	______	______	______

Part 4 Activities

21. Many people dream of owning their own business, but only a small percentage of people ever take the risk to become entrepreneurs. As you learned in this chapter, successful entrepreneurs have many personal characteristics in common. Answer each question below by placing a check mark in the *Yes* or *No* column to determine if you have what it takes to become a successful entrepreneur.

		Yes	No
1.	I am willing to spend long hours on business ideas that excite me.	________	________
2.	I am self-motivated and do not need other people to direct my work.	________	________
3.	I am willing to take reasonable risks to achieve my goals.	________	________
4.	I am not easily discouraged by failures and learn from my mistakes.	________	________
5.	I am well organized and manage my time wisely.	________	________
6.	I try to think outside of the box when seeking solutions to problems.	________	________
7.	The quality of my work is important to me.	________	________
8.	I am willing to seek advice from others who can help and guide me.	________	________
9.	I manage money carefully so that I can invest in business ideas.	________	________
10.	I have a strong desire to be the best in everything I undertake.	________	________

22. Arrange to interview several small business owners in your community. Prepare your list of questions prior to conducting the interviews. You may want to ask how they decided on the product or service they offer. What background or experience did they have prior to starting the business? How did they initially finance the business? What kind of research did they conduct? Compare their responses. What similarities and differences do you notice among the people that you interviewed?

23. Many small businesses fail because the owners have a good idea for a business, but they fail to establish a written plan to cover all of the major business activities. Investigate a business that you might like to start. By referring to the Elements of a Business Plan in Chapter 6, begin drafting a written plan for your new business. You will need to include a complete description of the business as well as a description of any competitors you might have. Your business plan also should analyze your customers and describe the operations and marketing plans for the business. Finally, your business plan should analyze your financial needs, both for starting and for growing the business.

Name ______________________ Class ______________ Date ______________

Chapter 7 Study Guide Management and Leadership

Part 1 Yes or No

Directions Indicate your answer to each of the following questions by placing a check mark on the line under *yes* or *no* at the right.

	Yes	*No*
1. Are planning, staffing, and controlling all functions of management?	______	______
2. Is communication with suppliers an internal communication?	______	______
3. Are core values guiding principles of the company?	______	______
4. Is it true that "Leaders are born and not made"?	______	______
5. Is strategic management a style in which the manager is more controlling?	______	______
6. Are mid-managers responsible for specific areas of operation in a business?	______	______
7. Do ethical business practices involve only the company's executives?	______	______
8. Is communication from one manager to another horizontal communication?	______	______

Part 2 Unscramble

Directions Unscramble the following vocabulary words that were discussed in Chapter 7.

	Answers
9. louvcarese (2 words)	9. ______________
10. funceelni	10. ______________
11. dearpilshe	11. ______________
12. stiche	12. ______________
13. gametannem	13. ______________
14. thanimoreolans (2 words)	14. ______________
15. ginlapnn	15. ______________

Part 3 Matching

Directions In the Answers column indicate which kind of influence is best described by each statement.

A. Position influence
B. Reward influence
C. Expert influence
D. Identify influence

	Answers
16. Other employees acknowledge that the person has specialized knowledge.	16. ______
17. Examples include money, job benefits, or recognition.	17. ______
18. Having authority over others results in positive responses to requests.	18. ______
19. Criticizing rather than praising employees is another way to exercise influence.	19. ______
20. Employees are more willing to support someone whom they trust and respect.	20. ______

Part 4 Activities

21. Most leaders possess characteristics that make them effective managers. Each of those leadership characteristics offers a benefit to employees. Below is a list of the characteristics of effective leaders that were discussed in this chapter. For each characteristic, write a statement describing how employees will benefit from their manager having that specific characteristic.

Understanding ____________________

Initiative ____________________

Dependability ____________________

Judgment ____________________

Objectivity ____________________

Confidence ____________________

Stability ____________________

Cooperation ____________________

Honesty ____________________

Courage ____________________

Communications ____________________

Intelligence ____________________

22. Visit the web site for Wal-Mart and review the company's Statement of Ethics, including its Guiding Ethical Principles. Make a list of the ethical concerns and situations that are specifically addressed in Wal-Mart's Statement of Ethics. What process is in place for employees to report ethical concerns and issues at work?
23. Arrange to "shadow" a manager at a local company and observe the various tasks that the manager performs during the work day. Take notes during your visit and compile a list of each activity in which the manager is involved. From your notes, prepare a report linking each observed activity with one of the five functions of management—planning, organizing, staffing, implementing, or controlling. Also, identify the management style(s) you observed the manager using throughout the day. If you observed more than one style, describe the circumstances in which each style was used.

Name ______________________ Class ______________ Date ______________

Chapter 8 Study Guide Human Resources, Culture, and Diversity

Part 1 Agree or Disagree

Directions Indicate whether you agree or disagree with each of the following statements by placing a check mark in the column at the right.

	Agree	Disagree
1. A blue-collar worker is employed in an office with a casual dress code.	______	______
2. A layoff is a type of termination due to a change in business conditions.	______	______
3. A cafeteria plan is an employee benefit involving company-paid meals.	______	______
4. A glass ceiling is an architectural style that provides an open look for offices.	______	______
5. Downsizing is designed to decrease costs and increase efficiency.	______	______
6. Family leave policies permit employees to take off for a birth or adoption.	______	______
7. Flextime allows employees flexibility in the time they begin and end work.	______	______
8. A permanent employee works in the same position for his entire career.	______	______

Part 2 Completion

Directions In the Answers column, write the word or words needed to complete each sentence.

		Answers
9. (?) involves the use of automation to increase productivity.	9.	______________
10. A work schedule of 30 or more hours describes a (?) employee.	10.	______________
11. When an employee receives a (?), she assumes more responsibility.	11.	______________
12. Formal negotiation between management and unions is known as (?).	12.	______________
13. People 16 and older who are employed or seeking work make up the (?).	13.	______________
14. Many jobs in the U.S. are being (?) to other countries due to lower costs.	14.	______________
15. Telecommuting is a popular form of (?).	15.	______________

Part 3 Forms of Compensation

Directions Indicate the type of compensation described by each statement by placing a check mark in the appropriate column at the right. (There may be more than one correct answer for each statement.)

	Time Wage	Straight Salary	Incentive Pay	Benefits
16. Employees receive a share of company profits.	______	______	______	______
17. An employee is paid $7.50 per hour worked.	______	______	______	______
18. A sales associate earns 10% of his total sales.	______	______	______	______
19. A clerk receives $500 per week plus paid vacation.	______	______	______	______
20. Employees earn $0.30 for each widget produced.	______	______	______	______

Part 4 Activities

21. Companies today offer a variety of fringe benefits to their employees. Each benefit offers value to employees. Some businesses allow employees to select benefits that meet their specific needs by using a cafeteria plan. Below is a list of common fringe benefits. For each benefit, write a statement that describes the value of the benefit to employees.

Fringe Benefit	Value to Employees
vacation time	____________________
health insurance	____________________
life insurance	____________________
employee savings plan	____________________
paid sick days off	____________________
flextime	____________________
retirement program	____________________
recreational facility	____________________
day care for employees' children	____________________
employee discount for store purchases	____________________

Which of the fringe benefits listed above would be most important to you? Why?

____

22. Conduct research on one of the following federal laws that relate in some way to human resources: Family and Medical Leave Act, Civil Rights Act of 1964, Age Discrimination and Employment Act of 1967, or Americans with Disabilities Act. Organize and present information on the law you have selected by preparing a PowerPoint presentation, poster, or other creative visual representation of the material.

23. Select a job in which you may be interested. Determine the requirements for obtaining employment in that position by reviewing the classified advertisements in one or more newspapers for a period of at least one week. How many jobs in your chosen field are advertised? What are the listed requirements for each position? Do most of the ads list the same or similar job requirements (such as education or prior work experience)? Visit the U.S. Bureau of Labor Statistics web site to locate employment projections for the position. If possible, also visit a job or career fair to learn more about job opportunities in your chosen position. Compile your research in a report that provides a detailed overview of the job opportunities in the position you have selected.

Name ______________________ Class ______________ Date ______________

Chapter 9 Study Guide Career Planning and Development

Part 1 True or False

Directions Place a *T* for True or an *F* for False in the Answers column to show whether each of the following statements is true or false.

	Answers
1. Scholarships, student loans, and work-study options are all types of financial aid programs.	1. ______
2. Abilities are natural, inborn aptitudes to do specific things.	2. ______
3. Work-related experience can be gained through volunteer and school activities.	3. ______
4. Informational interviews help you learn about specific careers by talking to workers.	4. ______
5. An experience-based resume highlights your abilities related to the job you are pursuing.	5. ______
6. If you expressed your appreciation during the interview, a follow-up letter is not necessary.	6. ______
7. Mobility is often necessary to pursue your chosen career.	7. ______
8. Your resume should always include a list of references.	8. ______

Part 2 Matching

Directions In the Answers column, write the letter that represents the word, or group of words, that correctly completes the statement.

		Answers
9. Spending a day or week with a worker to learn about a job	A. values	9. ______
10. Asks for employment-related information	B. networking	10. ______
11. An experienced employee who acts as a counselor	C. ability	11. ______
12. Things that are important to you	D. career portfolio	12. ______
13. Provides evidence of your ability and skills	E. job shadow	13. ______
14. Talking to other people about their jobs	F. mentor	14. ______
15. Being able to perform a mental or physical task	G. application form	15. ______
	H. resume	

Part 3 Types of Interviews

Directions Indicate the type of interview described by each statement by placing a check mark in the appropriate column at the right. (There may be more than one correct answer for each statement.)

	Informational Interview	Employment Interview	Exit Interview
16. Prepare in advance for questions you might be asked.	______	______	______
17. Learn more about the preparation needed for a career.	______	______	______
18. Answer questions honestly and completely.	______	______	______
19. Offer constructive feedback.	______	______	______
20. Thank the interviewer for his or her time and for the opportunity to discuss the job.	______	______	______

Part 4 Activities

21. Since your values affect your career plans directly or indirectly, it is a good idea to examine the personal values you hold. Read each value described in the list below. Then place a check mark in the column at the right that indicates the importance of that value to you.

VALUE	IMPORTANCE TO ME Very Important	 Important	 Not Important
Prestige—gaining recognition and status	________	________	________
Money—getting financial reward	________	________	________
Power—having control over people, money, or things	________	________	________
Achievement—accomplishing goals	________	________	________
Independence—controlling my time and actions	________	________	________
Security—having a stable work condition	________	________	________
Belonging—feeling I am part of a group	________	________	________
Serving others—doing things for others	________	________	________

List the three values that you consider to be the most important to you. State how each of these values might affect your career choice.

____

____

____

22. When applying for certain jobs, you may be required to complete the company's standard application form. For other jobs, however, you may need to provide the potential employer with a resume. Begin compiling relevant information that could be used to construct your resume, such as a statement of your career objective, education, work or volunteer experience, and any honors you have earned or activities in which you are involved. Once you have assembled all of the necessary information, prepare your resume using the sample resume in this chapter as a guide.

23. Review the list of common interview questions in this chapter, and write answers for each of the questions. Using a tape recorder, record your answers. Play the recording and make note of any answers that are not delivered in a clear, positive tone. Record those answers again and continue working to improve your delivery until you feel that you could answer each question confidently in an actual interview.

Name ______________________ Class ______________ Date ______________

DECISIONS, DECISIONS, DECISIONS—PART 1

A Decision-Making Project

As a consumer, worker, and citizen, you constantly make decisions that affect your future—both personally and financially. Some of these decisions are made very quickly while others require time, research, and careful deliberation.

In this project, you will make various personal and business decisions, based on your personal goals, values, and business knowledge. Each situation you will consider presents several choices you can make, but each choice will have financial consequences. Therefore, you should choose carefully. Random events that are based on chance also will affect you financially. The components of this project are:

DECISIONS: For each decision, you will have three alternatives from which to choose. You should consider not only the immediate effects of your decision but also how it will affect your future.

CONSEQUENCES: These are direct results of the decisions you will be making. Your teacher wiil provide you with the consequences as they are needed.

RANDOM EVENTS: Random events are beyond your control. However, they still can affect you financially. Cut out the numbered slips of paper below and place them in a bag or box. When instructed to do so, you will draw a number that will indicate how you will be affected by the random event.

After you have made your decision for each situation, you will record the financial result on the summary sheet at the end of the project. Each decision, consequence, or random event will either increase or decrease your balance. At the end of the project, calculate your final balance.

Your teacher will assign you to work individually or in a group. If you are assigned to work in a group, you should discuss your decisions with other group members and arrive at a shared decision.

1	2	3
4	5	6

[This page left intentionally blank]

Name ______________________ Class ______________ Date ______________

Situation 1—Decision—After High School

You have graduated from high school and must decide what you will do next. Keep in mind that your decision will affect future opportunities. Record the amount for your decision on your summary sheet.

Choice A	Choice B	Choice C
continue your education and work part-time	work full time at a local business	start your own business
+$7,000	**+$16,500**	**+$11,700**

Situation 2—Decision—Rent or Buy

You need to choose a place to live. You have a choice of renting or buying. Before you make your decision, you should investigate the advantages and disadvantages of each choice.

Choice A	Choice B	Choice C
rent an apartment, which requires a security deposit and first month's rent	buy a previously owned house, which requires a down payment	buy a new condominium, which requires a down payment
–$750	**–$4,800**	**–$2,600**

Situation 3—Random Event—Supply and Demand in Action

Due to recent economic conditions, the supply and/or demand of various products has changed. Select a number to determine which result affects you and record the amount on your summary sheet.

Result 1	Result 2	Result 3	Result 4	Result 5	Result 6
lower taxes, higher demand (prices up)	higher taxes, lower demand (prices down)	bad weather, reduced supply	new technology, increased supply	high government spending, increased demand	higher wages, higher demand
–$80	**–$50**	**–$120**	**–$100**	**–$90**	**–$60**

Situation 4—Decision—Selecting a Computer

Your business and personal needs require the use of a computer. Select a method for obtaining the use of a computer.

Choice A	Choice B	Choice C
purchase computer with monthly payment of **–$150**	rent computer with monthly charge of **–$200**	buy computer time from information processing service bureau for a monthly charge of **–$125**

Situation 5—Consequence—A Previous Decision

As a result of your decision in Situation 1, you will receive a salary increase. The amount of this increase must be obtained from your teacher. Be sure to record the amount of the increase on your summary sheet.

Situation 6—Random Event—Moving Expenses

Your recent move into a new home has resulted in various expenses—utility deposits, kitchen supplies and linens. Select a number to determine which result will affect you and record the amount on your summary sheet.

Result 1	Result 2	Result 3	Result 4	Result 5	Result 6
–$80	**–$50**	**–$120**	**–$100**	**–$90**	**–$60**

Situation 7—Decision—A Vote on Taxes

Your local government needs additional revenue for various community services. Carefully consider your options, and select one of the choices below.

Choice A	Choice B	Choice C
vote for a tax increase, which would maintain all current public services **–$200**	vote for a tax increase, which would maintain roads and schools at current levels but could result in a decrease in other public services **–$120**	vote against a tax increase, which could result in a decrease in numerous public services **NO COST**

Situation 8—Random Event—Interest Rates

Interest rates are always changing. Select a number to determine how the change in interest rates will affect you. Record the results on your summary sheet.

Result 1	Result 2	Result 3	Result 4	Result 5	Result 6
increased money supply, rates fall	lower money supply, rates rise	increased demand for loans, rates rise	lower demand for loans, rates fall	higher wages and spending, rates rise	decreased government borrowing, rates fall
+$50	**–$40**	**–$70**	**+$80**	**–$60**	**+$70**

Situation 9—Decision—Additional Career Training

You must decide whether or not you will pursue additional education. Record your choice on your summary sheet.

Choice A	Choice B	Choice C
obtain advanced training in your chosen career	obtain training in another career area with a good occupational outlook for the future	obtain no additional training at this time
–$400	**–$900**	**NO COST**

Situation 10—Consequence—Computer Costs

As a result of your decision in Situation 4, your computer costs have been influenced by various factors. See your teacher for the results of this situation. Be sure to record the amount on your summary sheet.

Situation 11—Random Event—Salary Increase

As a result of your time and effort on the job, you qualify for a pay increase. Select a number to determine the amount. Record the results on your summary sheet.

Result 1	Result 2	Result 3	Result 4	Result 5	Result 6
+$80	+$50	+$160	+$100	+$30	+$120

Situation 12—Decision—Product Purchase

You have decided to buy a television for your new home. Choose one of the following and record its cost on your summary sheet. You may want to investigate each option carefully before making your decision.

Choice A	Choice B	Choice C
a well-known national brand	a store brand	an unknown brand
–$600	**–$450**	**–$300**

Situation 13—Random Event—Computer Time Savings

As a result of recent developments, a cost savings has been created related to your computer. Select a number to determine the amount of the savings. Record the results on your summary sheet.

Result 1	Result 2	Result 3	Result 4	Result 5	Result 6
+$70	+$40	+$90	+$50	+$120	+$150

Situation 14—Consequence—Home Repair

The driveway of your home is in need of repair. Based on the decision you made in Situation 2, obtain the amount of this repair from your teacher. Be sure to record the amount of the increase on your summary sheet.

Name ______________________ Class ______________ Date ______________

Situation 15—Decision—Foreign Trade

The company for which you work must decide where it wants to expand sales. You must make the decision.

Choice A	Choice B	Choice C
expand foreign business, maintain current level of domestic business	expand level of domestic operations; no foreign business	expand both foreign and domestic business operations
–$600	–$300	–$750

Situation 16—Consequence—Training Results

As a result of your decision in Situation 9, your salary level has been affected. See your teacher for the results of this situation. Be sure to record the amount on your summary sheet.

Situation 17—Decision—New Career Choice

You are considering a career change. Certain costs would be involved due to moving and training expenses. Record your choice on the summary sheet.

Choice A	Choice B	Choice C
select a new career in a field related to your present job	select a new career in a different field of work	maintain the same career as presently held
–$400	–$850	NO COST

Situation 18—Random Event—Changing Government Services

Because of economic conditions, government tax revenues have decreased and some government services have been reduced. Consumers must now pay for some services that were previously provided. Select a number to determine how you will be affected.

Result 1	Result 2	Result 3	Result 4	Result 5	Result 6
–$20	–$50	–$30	–$70	–$40	–$20

Situation 19—Consequence—Television Repair

The television you purchased in Situation 12 is in need of repair. See your teacher for the costs involved. Be sure to record the amount on your summary sheet.

Situation 20—Decision—Store Choice

You have decided to purchase your clothing on a regular basis at one of the types of stores listed. Record your choice on your summary sheet.

Choice A	Choice B	Choice C
full-service department store located 8 miles away	full-service local specialty store located 3 miles away	factory outlet located 13 miles away
–$70	**–$90**	**–$60**

Situation 21—Consequence—Computer Repair

Due to heavy usage, the computer you selected in Situation 4 needs to be repaired. See your teacher for the results of this situation. Record the amount on your summary sheet.

Situation 22—Decision—Type of Business Organization

You have decided to start your own business. Now you must decide which of the three basic business structures you will use. Record your choice on your summary sheet.

Choice A	Choice B	Choice C
sole proprietorship with organizational costs of	partnership with organizational costs of	corporation with organizational costs of
–$150	**–$250**	**–$500**

Situation 23—Consequence—Clothing Costs

As a result of your decision in Situation 20, obtain the amount of your clothing costs from your teacher. Be sure to record the amount on your summary sheet.

Name ______________________ Class ______________ Date ______________

Situation 24—Random Event—Economic Conditions

As a result of a depressed economy, you are unemployed for a length of time. Select a number to determine the amount of salary you have lost. Record the results on your summary sheet.

Result 1	Result 2	Result 3	Result 4	Result 5	Result 6
–$300	–$500	–$370	–$280	–$440	–$340

Situation 25—Consequence—Government Costs

Certain government services have been affected by the recent tax vote in Situation 7. See your teacher for the results. Be sure to record the amount on your summary sheet.

Situation 26—Random Event—Profit or Loss

Your involvement with a business in Situation 22 has resulted in a profit or loss. To determine which you will receive, select a number. Record the results on your summary sheet.

Result 1	Result 2	Result 3	Result 4	Result 5	Result 6
profit +$700	profit +$450	loss –$550	loss –$300	loss –$320	profit +$560

Situation 27—Consequence—Housing Equity
See your teacher regarding increased value of your property resulting from your decision in Situation 2. Record the amount on your summary sheet.

Situation 28—Consequence—New Career Success
See your teacher regarding a possible salary increase resulting from your career decision in Situation 17. Record the amount on your summary sheet.

Situation 29—Consequence—Business Ownership and Expansion
See your teacher regarding the results of your choices made in Situations 15 and 22.

Name ______________________ Class ______________ Date ______________

DECISIONS, DECISIONS, DECISIONS—PART 1—SUMMARY SHEET

	SITUATION	TOPIC	CHOICE	AMOUNT	BALANCE
1.	Decision	After High School	______	+ ______	______
2.	Decision	Rent or Buy	______	– ______	______
3.	Random Event	Supply and Demand in Action	______	– ______	______
4.	Decision	Selecting a Computer	______	– ______	______
5.	Consequence	A Previous Decision		+ ______	______
6.	Random Event	Moving Expenses	______	– ______	______
7.	Decision	A Vote on Taxes	______	– ______	______
8.	Random Event	Interest Rates	______	+/– ______	______
9.	Decision	Additional Career Training	______	– ______	______
10.	Consequence	Computer Costs		+/– ______	______
11.	Random Event	Salary Increase	______	+ ______	______
12.	Decision	Product Purchase	______	– ______	______
13.	Random Event	Computer Time Savings	______	+ ______	______
14.	Consequence	Home Repair		– ______	______
15.	Decision	Foreign Trade	______	– ______	______
16.	Consequence	Training Results		+ ______	______
17.	Decision	New Career Choice	______	– ______	______
18.	Random Event	Changing Government Services	______	– ______	______
19.	Consequence	Television Repair		– ______	______
20.	Decision	Store Choice	______	– ______	______
21.	Consequence	Computer Repair		– ______	______
22.	Decision	Type of Business Organization	______	– ______	______
23.	Consequence	Clothing Costs		– ______	______
24.	Random Event	Economic Conditions	______	– ______	______
25.	Consequence	Government Costs		– ______	______
26.	Random Event	Profit or Loss	______	+/– ______	______
27.	Consequence	Housing Equity		+ ______	______
28.	Consequence	New Career Success		+ ______	______
29.	Consequence	Business Ownership and Expansion	(a)	+ ______	______
			(b)	– ______	______
				FINAL BALANCE	______

Student Comments:

1. Which decisions might you have made differently? Why?

2. What factors did you forget to consider when making a decision?

3. What advice would you give to someone about making financial decisions?